PLAN OF GARDEN

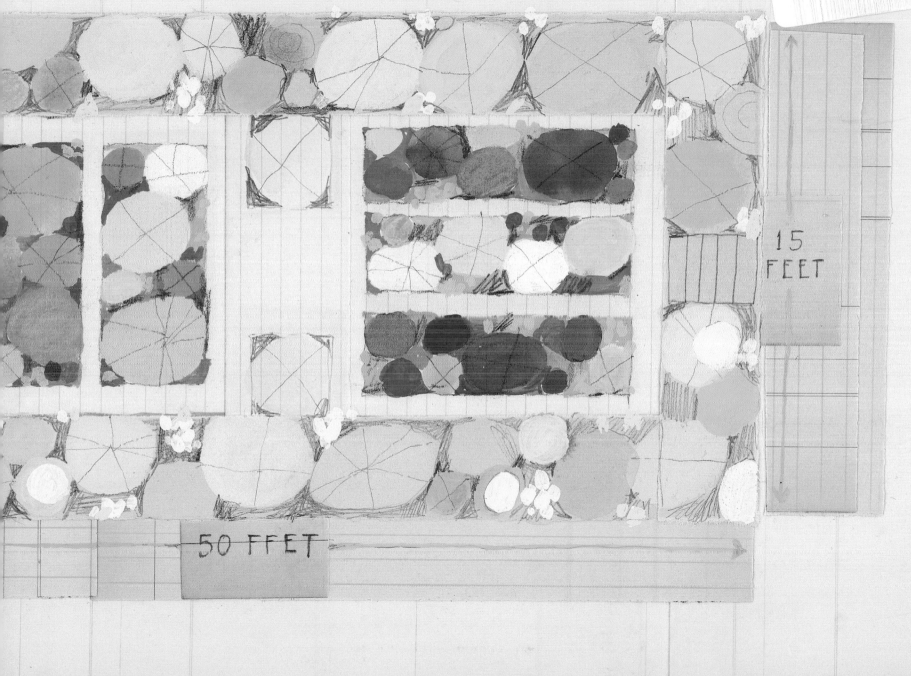

15 FEET

50 FFET

CELIA PLANTED A GARDEN

THE STORY OF CELIA THAXTER AND HER ISLAND GARDEN

Phyllis Root & Gary D. Schmidt

illustrated by Melissa Sweet

CANDLEWICK PRESS

When Celia Laighton was very young, she lived on White Island, where the rocks were gray and white, and the waves that broke on the rocks were gray and white, and the seagulls that rode the sea were gray and white.

So in the spring, Celia planted a garden between rocky ledges, bright with yellow marigolds.

EVER SINCE I COULD REMEMBER ANYTHING, FLOWERS HAVE BEEN LIKE DEAR FRIENDS TO ME.

During the summer, while her father kept the island lighthouse, Celia and her brothers played by the shore, where pink morning glories opened to the sun, and Celia found green moss and purple starfish in rocky pools. When the scarlet pimpernel flowers closed their petals, Celia knew a storm was on its way.

THE
LITTLE
SCARLET
PIMPERNEL
CHARMED ME.

IT SEEMED MORE
THAN A **FLOWER**;

IT WAS LIKE A
HUMAN THING.

In the fall, she waved at the birds migrating south over the island to their winter homes—blue-winged swallows and olive-brown thrushes and red-chested robins and yellow warblers and black-capped nuthatches and scarlet tanagers and golden orioles and rusty sandpipers. Even at night they flew while the beams from the lighthouse flashed red and white, red and white, red and white.

In the winter, Celia and her brothers warmed pennies with their breath and held them against the windows to melt peepholes in the frost so they could see the wild gray waves and the blowing white snow.

THE SEA IS BLACK AND WHITE AS DEATH, WITH HORRIBLE LONG BILLOWS THAT BREAK AND ROAR ALOUD.

One fierce winter storm blew away the island's boathouses. Another washed the henhouse out to sea. Another blew through the windows and flung down their dishes from the shelves. Celia's father brought Betsy, their cow, into the kitchen to keep her from being washed away too!

MORE DEAR TO ME THAN WORDS CAN TELL WAS EVERY CUP AND SPRAY AND LEAF; TOO PERFECT FOR A LIFE SO BRIEF SEEMED EVERY STAR AND BUD AND BELL.

But spring always came, and the summer birds returned, and Celia planted a garden.

THE VERY ACT OF PLANTING A SEED IN THE EARTH HAS IN IT TO ME SOMETHING BEAUTIFUL.

When she was twelve, Celia and her family moved to nearby Appledore Island. While her father built a large hotel, Celia searched for patches of soil among the bare rocks and looked for springs to water her new garden, but she found only the fresh water that came from the rains.

Still, Celia planted a bigger garden than before, even though she had so much to do at the new hotel. Artists and writers were coming to stay, and each summer day she greeted the new guests and went out to plant. She served in the hotel's dining room and went out to weed. She made up the guests' beds and went out to clip blossoms for the vases on their dressers.

And on that rocky and waterless island, Celia's garden bloomed gloriously.

Celia grew older, and her garden grew larger, and one day, Celia met Levi Thaxter. Levi was afraid of the sea, and he did not like Appledore Island very much. When they married, they moved to the mainland to raise their family.

I LONG FOR

THE LIGHT AND
LIFE, AND
EVER-SHIFTING
COLOR, AND
EVER-DELICIOUS
SOUND
OF THE FAITHFUL
OLD SEA
MORE IN THE
WINTER
THAN IN THE
SUMMER.

But during the long wintry days, when the low clouds were gray and the ground was frosted white with snow, Celia missed the tumbled shores of her island home, and the rising and falling tides, and the crash of the waves on the rocks—and her garden.

So Celia wrote poems about Appledore Island and the sea around it, and her words opened like flowers. The people Celia met on the island published her poems in magazines and books so that any reader could imagine what it was like to live far out in the ocean, on a rocky island, with the sounds of the waves and the sea breezes tossing the garden flowers. Her poems even gave hope to ice-wrecked arctic explorers who brought them along on their expedition.

TO FEEL THE WIND, SEA-SCENTED,
ON MY CHEEK,
TO CATCH THE SOUND OF
DUSKY FLAPPING SAIL
AND DIP OF OARS, AND VOICES
ON THE GALE
AFAR OFF, CALLING LOW, --
MY NAME THEY SPEAK!

And while she wrote, Celia filled her windowsills with passionflowers, pink and yellow roses, red geraniums, and white calla lilies. She started seeds in eggshells—bright pansies and asters and cup-and-saucer vines. She put them in the sunlight that shone through her bay windows.

And Celia painted what she remembered from her island summers. She painted the sea and top-masted sailboats. She painted purple irises on greeting cards. White china pitchers and bowls and plates bloomed with shy asters and loud poppies under Celia's brush.

POST CARD

Levi Cooley,
333 Charles Street
Boston,
Massachusetts

THIS SPACE FOR WRITING MESSAGES

I WANT
TO PAINT
EVERYTHING
I SEE;
EVERY LEAF,
STEM, SEED
VESSEL, GRASS
BLADE, RUSH, AND
REED AND
FLOWER
HAS NEW CHARMS,
AND I THOUGHT
I KNEW THEM
ALL BEFORE.

THE
SONG SPARROWS
FILL THE HOUSE,
THEY FLY INTO
THE GREAT
RAMBLING
EMPTY PLACE
AND
SING,
OH HOW THEY
SING!
THE SWEETEST CHEERFUL
SONGS,
ALL DAY AND ABOUT
ALL NIGHT...

In the springtime, after long winters, Celia sailed back to Appledore, carrying the seedlings to plant her garden. Year after year, she planted. She planted pansies, sweet peas and hollyhocks, dark larkspurs and foxgloves, and tall sunflowers and red dahlias and nasturtiums and golden California poppies—and yellow marigolds. All summer long the flowers blossomed and brightened the island, pretty as a poem, pretty as a painting. All summer long the birds were at home in her garden—and even her house.

But storms come in summer too.

One night, a storm threw salt waves high upon the rocks and lightning zigzagged the sky. The wind thrashed the flowers in the garden and freezing rain poured down.

THE BOATS TOSS MADLY ON THE MOORINGS, THE SEA BREAKS WILDLY ON THE SHORE, THE WORLD IS DROWNED AND GONE. THERE IS NOTHING BUT TEMPEST AND TUMULT AND RUSH AND ROAR OF WIND AND RAIN.

The next morning, when Celia came out at "bird-peep," she found a hummingbird
frozen, his ruby chest still, his claws clinging to the stem of a flattened red poppy.
The storm had blown him all the way out to Appledore Island.

Celia cupped the hummingbird in her hand and breathed her warm breath over
his soft feathers. Nothing. She carried the tiny body in the nest of her hand as she
gathered the broken flowers. Again she breathed on the tiny body. Nothing.
She breathed again and again.

Then Celia felt a small flutter of a heartbeat. She breathed over the hummingbird again.
A stirring of wings! She breathed again. The hummingbird opened his eyes! So gently,
Celia placed him in a little basket lined with soft wool and hung it in the sunshine.
Soon the hummingbird flew up into the light and dove toward a blue larkspur to feed.

It was as if the hummingbird had come home—just where he should be. In Celia's garden.

That summer, the hummingbird flitted through the garden, sipping from flowers that Celia held in her hand, showering in the raindrops that dripped from the sweet pea blossoms.

Fall came, and Celia cleared the sticks and stalks from her garden. She dug up the dahlia bulbs and wayward hollyhocks. She covered the ground with dark manure.

THE MARTINS ALMOST LIGHT ON MY HEAD; THE HUMMINGBIRDS DO, AND TANGLE THEIR LITTLE CLAWS IN MY HAIR; SO DO THE SPARROWS.

I GATHER THE SEED-PODS IN THE GARDEN BEDS, SHARING THEIR BOUNTY WITH THE BIRDS I LOVE SO WELL.

And when the birds flew away to winter homes,
Celia sailed to the mainland.

Until next spring.

A NOTE ON
CELIA LAIGHTON THAXTER

In the middle of her most famous poem, "Land-Locked," Celia Thaxter wrote, "Have patience,—here are flowers and songs of birds, / Beauty and fragrance, wealth of sound and sight, / All summer's glory thine from morn till night, / And life too full of joy for uttered words." If Celia Thaxter were to summarize her entire life in a single stanza, she might have chosen this one. Her life was surrounded by flowers and birds, by the sounds of the sea and the wind, and, it seems, by summer. When she wrote these lines, she wasn't living on her island—but she was clearly thinking about it.

Born in Portsmouth, New Hampshire, she moved to the Isles of Shoals when her father became the lighthouse keeper of White Island—a tiny island so barren and inhospitable that it is still hard to reach today. By the time she was twelve, her family had moved to Hog Island, which her father renamed Appledore Island—the name by which it is still known. Isolated from the mainland by seven miles of ocean, Celia and her brothers, Cedric and Oscar, grew up exploring their island world until they were old enough to help tend the lighthouse and, after her father built a hotel, tend guests.

The hotel brought the world to Celia. Attractive because of both its ocean views and the supposed health benefits of the sea air, the hotel gathered great writers and artists from all over New England, including the poets Henry Wadsworth Longfellow and John Greenleaf Whittier and the novelist Nathaniel Hawthorne—along with his publisher, who invited Celia to submit her poetry to his magazine, the *Atlantic Monthly*. "Land-Locked" was her first submission, but many others followed, and she became one of the best-known poets of her time, though today she is considered principally a regional poet. Publishers encouraged Celia to write about her childhood in *Among the Isles of Shoals* (1873) and then to write about her garden on Appledore in *An Island Garden* (1894), a book illustrated by another guest at the Appledore hotel, the impressionist painter Childe Hassam. Celia died a few months after its publication.

An Island Garden remains one of her most famous works, and though her poetry is still anthologized, and her paintings and ceramic decoration still prized, it is her account of her garden that is her chief fame. Today, though the buildings she knew on Appledore burned down over a century ago, the garden has been re-created on the island on which she is buried, and with which she will forever be linked.

1835   June 29: Celia Laighton is born to parents Thomas Laighton and Eliza Rymes.

1839   Thomas Laighton purchases Smuttynose, Malaga, Hog, and Cedar Islands. His family moves to White Island, where Thomas is the keeper of the lighthouse.

Celia's brother Oscar is born. He will never live off the Isles of Shoals.

1840   Celia's second brother, Cedric, is born. He will leave the islands only after his marriage.

1841   Thomas is elected to the House of Representatives for the New Hampshire legislature, and the family leaves White Island for Smuttynose Island, where Eliza transforms their large house into an inn.

1846   July: Levi Thaxter comes to board with the Laighton family on Smuttynose Island; in the fall, he becomes the children's tutor.

1847   The Laightons move to Hog Island, and Thomas builds a resort hotel with the help of Levi Thaxter, Celia's future husband. They rename the ninety-five-acre island Appledore Island.

1848   June 15: Appledore House opens to the public.

1849   Celia spends a semester at the Mount Washington Female Seminary in Boston, her only formal education.

1851   September 30: Celia (sixteen years old) and Levi Thaxter marry in the front parlor of Appledore House. They move to Watertown, Massachusetts.

1852   Summer: Celia and Levi return to Appledore for the birth of their son, Karl. After a few months, they discern that Karl may have cerebral palsy.

September: Nathaniel Hawthorne visits Appledore House and is later joined by Franklin Pierce.

1854   While living in Newburyport, Massachusetts, Celia has her second son, John.

1855   Fall: While sailing, Celia's brother Oscar and her husband are almost drowned in a sudden storm; Levi vows never to return to Appledore, though he would years later. Celia, however, continues to return regularly.

1856   The Thaxter family moves to Newtonville, outside of Boston, into the first home they have owned.

1858   January: Celia's brother Cedric makes his first journey off Appledore Island to visit Celia and her family. He sees his first mature trees and quickly returns to the island.

August: Celia's third son, Roland, is born. The family will call him "Lony" for his entire life; he was said to be the favorite child.

1860   Despite summer visits to Appledore, Celia becomes more and more homesick for her island home.

1861   March: Celia Thaxter's poem "Land-Locked" is published in America's most prestigious literary magazine, the *Atlantic Monthly*, introducing her to the publishing house of Ticknor and Fields.

1863   Celia Thaxter receives a visit in Newtonville from her publisher, James Fields, and his wife, Annie; they become close friends.

Roland and John begin to take vacations with their father while Celia and Karl return to Appledore, signaling the separate lives that divided the Thaxter family.

1866   Thomas Laighton, Celia Thaxter's father, dies, leaving the island property to his sons and his wife; Celia receives $5,200, to be paid out by her brothers in installments.

1867   January: Celia and Levi Thaxter attend a dinner party hosted by the Fields— and including Charles Dickens and Henry Wadsworth Longfellow.

April: The Fields host another dinner party, this time including Longfellow again, as well as Ralph Waldo Emerson and Oliver Wendell Holmes—signaling Celia's entry into the American literary world.

1868   "The Wreck of the Pocahontas" is published. One of Celia Thaxter's early popular poems, is was inspired by a shipwreck she witnessed from White Island.

The Thaxters adopt Ignatius Grossman, a Hungarian immigrant about fifteen years old at the time.

1869   The family begins a distinct pattern of separation; Levi would take their two younger sons to travel and Celia would return to Appledore Island with Karl.

1869–70   Urged on by James Fields, Celia Thaxter writes a series of articles about her island home.

1872   *Poems* is published; many of the pieces had already been published in the *Atlantic*. The volume includes "Sandpiper," one of her most popular poems.

1873	*Among the Isles of Shoals* is published, following articles published in the *Atlantic* about Appledore Island.
1874	*Poems* is published. It is Celia Thaxter's second collection of poetry, though it has the same title as the first.
1877	Celia begins to paint floral arrangements and designs on china as well as watercolor landscapes as a distraction during her mother's decline; this art will continue the rest of her life.

November 19: Celia's mother, Eliza, dies. |
| 1879 | *Drift-Weed* is published. |
| 1880 | Celia returns to Appledore Island virtually full-time, establishing a literary salon there that attracts artists from around the country.

August: Sarah Orne Jewett visits Appledore House. She and Annie Fields and Celia Thaxter will become very close friends.

The family sells the Newtonville house and purchases Champernowne Farm in Kittery, Maine, both to provide a vocation as a dairy farmer for John and to plan for a future home for Karl. On a clear day, the view from the farm included Appledore Island.

Levi and Celia Thaxter come to agree that they will live apart. Levi begins to give public readings; Celia sails to Europe with her brother Oscar. When they return, Celia moves into a Boston apartment with Karl during the winter and then moves to Appledore Island for the rest of the year. This pattern continues for the remainder of her life. |
| 1881 | Childe Hassam visits Appledore House for the first time. |
| 1883 | *Stories and Poems for Children* is published. |
| 1884 | May 31: Levi Thaxter dies and is buried at Kittery Point.

John begins a serious career as a dairyman. |
| 1886 | *The Cruise of the Mystery, and Other Poems* is published.

Idyls and Pastorals: A Home Gallery of Poetry and Art is published.

Childe Hassam begins his Appledore paintings.

Celia Thaxter becomes the secretary of the Audubon Society in Waltham, Massachusetts, and begins vigorous advocacy for birdlife. |
1887	John marries Mary Gertrude Stoddard, whose personal wealth will help support the family and dairy business. Their daughter Rosamond will write a biography of her grandmother: *Sandpiper: The Life and Letters of Celia Thaxter*.
1888	Roland receives his PhD in entomology from Harvard University, where he will later serve as a professor. In this year, he marries Mabel Freeman, and together they will raise four children, giving Celia what she says is her greatest happiness.
1889	*Yule Log* is published.
1890	*My Lighthouse, and Other Poems* is published.

Childe Hassam visits Appledore Island again. He will continue to visit each year until Celia Thaxter's death. |
| 1891 | *Verses* is published.

Celia begins to battle both poor health and depression. |
| 1894 | *An Island Garden* is published.

August 25, at dawn: Celia Thaxter dies suddenly. She is fifty-nine years old. She is buried on the island in a coffin filled with flowers. |
1895	Annie Fields and Rose Lamb publish *Letters of Celia Thaxter, Edited by Her Friends*.
1899	*The Poems of Celia Thaxter* is published.
1910	The United States Coast Guard builds a life-saving station on Appledore Island.
1914	The Appledore Hotel burns down, a complete loss.
1928	The University of New Hampshire's Department of Zoology establishes its Marine Zoological Laboratory on Appledore Island.
1935	Oscar Laighton's edited collection of Celia Thaxter's work, *The Heavenly Guest with Other Unpublished Writings*, is published.
1940	Appledore Island is occupied by United States military observers during World War II. When they leave, the island remains mostly unoccupied, the buildings there decaying and falling prey to vandals.
1973	The Shoals Marine Laboratory is established on Appledore Island.
1977	Under the direction of John Kingsbury, the Shoals Marine Laboratory restores Celia Thaxter's garden as she had described and mapped it in *An Island Garden*.

Bibliography

Brown, Nell Porter. "Time Apart." *Harvard Magazine*, March–April 2017, 16H–16L. A brief history of Appledore, including current use.

Curry, David. *Childe Hassam: An Island Garden Revisited.* New York: W. W. Norton, 1990. This well-illustrated volume, which accompanied an exhibition of Hassam's work, focuses on the ways in which his use of light and color were strongly affected by Celia Thaxter's gardens.

Fields, Annie. *Authors and Friends.* Boston: Houghton Mifflin, 1896. A collection of memories about friends who attended the salon that Annie Fields maintained, even long after the death of her husband, the publisher James Fields.

Fields, Annie, ed. *Letters of Sarah Orne Jewett.* Boston: Houghton Mifflin, 1911. An edited collection of letters that includes correspondence between Celia Thaxter and the New England writer Sarah Orne Jewett.

Fields, Annie, and Rose Lamb, eds. *Letters of Celia Thaxter, Edited by Her Friends.* Boston: Houghton Mifflin, 1895. In addition to offering a very loving biography of Celia Thaxter, this book collects extracts from Thaxter's many letters from 1856 through 1894, noting the island's harsh winters, the coming of birds and flowers and butterflies, and the storms that tore at the island's shores.

Hill, May Brawley. *Grandmother's Garden: The Old-Fashioned American Garden, 1865–1915.* New York: Harry N. Abrams, 1995. In this general study of turn-of-the-century gardens, Hill devotes ten pages to Celia Thaxter's work and provides one of the more easily accessible ways to see the work of artists inspired by Thaxter's Appledore garden.

Howe, M. A. DeWolfe. *Memories of a Hostess: A Chronicle of Eminent Friendships.* Boston: The Atlantic Monthly Press, 1922. These "memories" are drawn from the diaries of Mrs. Annie Fields, whose first name is never mentioned in the book. Her husband was one of the two partners in Ticknor and Fields, which published Celia Thaxter's work.

Laighton, Cedric. *Letters to Celia: Written During the Years 1860–1875 to Celia Laighton Thaxter by Her Brother Cedric Laighton.* Edited and illustrated by Frederick T. McGill. Boston: Star Island, 1972.

Laighton, Oscar. *Ninety Years at the Isles of Shoals.* Boston: Beacon Press, 1930. Reprint, Boston: Star Island, 1988. The memoir of Celia Thaxter's beloved brother.

Laighton, Oscar, ed. *The Heavenly Guest with Other Unpublished Writings.* Edited by Oscar Laighton. Andover, MA: Smith and Coutts, 1935. The last collection of unpublished writings by Celia Thaxter, along with reprinted pieces by some of her friends and acquaintances.

Mandel, Norma H. *Beyond the Garden Gate: The Life of Celia Laighton Thaxter.* Hanover, NH: University Press of New England, 2004. A biography that draws on previously unpublished letters and that focuses on the import of her isolated childhood and early marriage.

Martin, Tovah. "An Artist's Garden by the Sea." *Gardener*, Summer 2004, 76–79.

———. "Celia Thaxter's Island Garden." *Country Gardens*, Early Spring (January) 2014, 30–35.

Older, Julia. *The Island Queen.* Hancock, NH: Appledore Books, 1994. A novelization of the life of Celia Thaxter on her island.

Parloa, Maria. *The Appledore Cook Book: Containing Practical Receipts for Plain and Rich Cooking.* Boston: Graves and Ellis, 1872. Parloa was one of the founders of the science of home economics, and early in her career she was one of the cooks at the Appledore hotel.

Rutledge, Lyman. *The Isles of Shoals in Lore and Legend.* Barre, MA: Barre Publishers, 1965. Reprint, Boston: Star Island, 1971.

Stearns, Frank Preston. *Sketches from Concord and Appledore.* New York: G. P. Putnam's Sons, 1895. Stearns was familiar with many of the writers that Celia Thaxter knew, and here he gives intimate portraits of those writers while visiting them in Concord, Massachusetts, and on the island with Celia Thaxter's family.

Stephan, Sharon Paiva. *One Woman's Work: The Visual Art of Celia Laighton Thaxter.* Portsmouth, NH: Portsmouth Athenaeum, 2001. A collection of essays to accompany a traveling exhibition of Thaxter's art, this volume is particularly useful for the many photographs of her art on porcelain and paper.

Thaxter, Celia. *Among the Isles of Shoals.* Boston: James R. Osgood, 1873. This is Celia Thaxter's most famous work, written at the desire of her many summer visitors.

———. *The Cruise of the Mystery, and Other Poems*. Boston: Houghton Mifflin, 1886.

———. *Drift-Weed*. Boston: Houghton, Osgood, 1879.

———. *Idyls and Pastorals: A Home Gallery of Poetry and Art*. Boston: D. Lothrop, 1886.

———. *An Island Garden*. Boston: Houghton Mifflin, 1894. Illustrated by Childe Hassam. Celia Thaxter's last and best-written book, focusing on her garden work on Appledore Island, with illustrations by one of America's most famous impressionist painters. The book was reprinted in 1988, again by Houghton Mifflin.

———. *My Lighthouse, and Other Poems*. Boston: L. Prang, 1890.

———. *Poems*. New York: Hurd and Houghton, 1872.

———. *The Poems of Celia Thaxter*. Boston: Houghton Mifflin, 1899.

———. *Stories and Poems for Children*. Boston: Houghton Mifflin, 1883.

———. *Verses*. Boston: Lathrop, 1891.

———. *Yule Log*. Boston: L. Prang, 1889.

Thaxter, Rosamond. *Sandpiper: The Life and Letters of Celia Thaxter and Her Home on the Isles of Shoals*. Francestown, NH: Marshall Jones, 1963. A collection of letters and reminiscences edited and written by Celia Thaxter's granddaughter. "Sandpiper" refers to a nickname given to Celia by Sarah Orne Jewett and to Thaxter's poem of the same name.

Titus, Donna Marion, ed. *By This Wing: Letters by Celia Thaxter to Bradford Torrey*. Manchester, NH: J. Palmer, 1999. Bradford Torrey—a Henry David Thoreau enthusiast—was a very prominent nature writer and bird-watcher, the most popular of Houghton Mifflin's authors writing about the outdoors.

Vallier, Jane E. *Poet on Demand: The Life, Letters and Works of Celia Thaxter*. Camden, ME: Down East Books, 1982. A literary biography of Celia Thaxter, focusing on the influence of the landscape on her writing.

All handwritten quotations in this book are taken from Celia Thaxter's own writings.

For Mary Rockcastle, who helps so many writers grow
PR and GDS

To Robin, whose garden is as pretty as a poem
MS

Text copyright © 2022 by Phyllis Root and Gary D. Schmidt
Illustrations copyright © 2022 by Melissa Sweet

First edition 2022

Library of Congress Catalog Card Number pending
ISBN 978-1-5362-0429-2

22 23 24 25 26 27 APS 10 9 8 7 6 5 4 3 2 1

Printed in Humen, Dongguan, China

This book was typeset in Weiss.
The illustrations were done in watercolor, gouache, and mixed media.

Candlewick Press
99 Dover Street
Somerville, Massachusetts 02144

www.candlewick.com